ECPE MICHIGAN PROFICIENCY ESSAY TEST SUCCESS: STUDY GUIDE WITH ESSAY PRACTICE TESTS AND WRITING SAMPLES

Examination for the Certificate of Proficiency in English and ECPE are registered trademarks of Michigan Language Assessment, in conjunction with Cambridge Assessment English, which are neither affiliated with nor endorse this publication.

ECPE Michigan Proficiency Essay Test Success: Study Guide with Essay Practice Tests and Writing Samples

Copyright © 2013, 2019 Academic Success Group DBA www.michigan-test.com.

All rights reserved. No part of this publication may be reproduced, stored in a retrieval system, or transmitted, in any form or by any means, electronic, mechanical, photocopying, recording, or otherwise.

ISBN-13: 978-1-949282-47-4

For information on bulk discounts, please contact us at: info@michigan-test.com

Examination for the Certificate of Proficiency in English and ECPE are registered trademarks of Michigan Language Assessment, in conjunction with Cambridge Assessment English, which are neither affiliated with nor endorse this publication.

COPYRIGHT NOTICE TO EDUCATORS

Please respect copyright law. Under no circumstances may you make copies of these materials for distribution to or use by students. Should you wish to use the materials with students, you are required to purchase a copy of this publication for each of your students.

TABLE OF CONTENTS

ECPE essay format and question types	1
ECPE essay scoring	3
How to avoid common errors on your essay	5
ECPE Essay Structure	7
Formulating Your Assertion	8
Supporting and Sustaining Your Argument	11
Acknowledging and Refuting the Counterargument	14
Extending and Elaborating Your Argument	17
Synthesizing the Viewpoints	19
Writing Your Conclusion	20
Sample essay 1	22
ECPE essays: The key points summed up	25
Organizing your ECPE essay	26
What is "argumentative language"?	28
Argumentative language exercise	29
Answer to argumentative language exercise	31
Using linking words and phrases effectively in your ECPE essay	34
Linking word exercise	39
Answers to the linking words exercise	42
Sample essay 2	42
Using adjectives to assert your opinion	45
Using adjectives - exercise	45
Answers to the adjective exercise	47
Using modality to argue your case	48
Modality exercise	48
Answers to the modality exercise	50

Using qualifiers to strengthen or limit your assertions	51
Qualifiers – exercise	51
Answers to the qualifiers exercise	52
Using verbs in the argument and counterargument	53
Verbs – exercise	53
List of verbs for the argument and counterargument	55
Answers to the verb exercise	57
Practice test 3	58
Answer to practice test 3 - sample essay 3	59
Analysis of essay structure in sample essay 3	62
Analysis of linking words and verbs in sample essay 3	64
Analysis of modality and qualifiers in sample essay 3	67
Practice test 4	70
Answer to practice test 4 - sample essay 4	71
Analysis of essay structure in sample essay 4	74
Analysis of linking words and verbs in sample essay 4	76
Analysis of modality and qualifiers in sample essay 4	79
Practice test 5	82
Answer to practice test 5 - sample essay 5	83
Analysis of essay structure in sample essay 5	86
Analysis of linking words and verbs in sample essay 5	89
Analysis of modality and qualifiers in sample essay 5	92
Vocabulary for the ECPE Essay – Using the Academic Word List	95
Academic Word List	96
ECPE Essay Writing – Practice Test Questions	103
Using Correct Grammar and Punctuation	105
Grammar and Punctuation – Exercises	115
Grammar and Punctuation – Answers	117

ECPE Essay Format & Question Types

ECPE Essay Assessment

Your ECPE testing assessment will include a written essay. The purpose of the essay is to assess your ability to express your thoughts in a well-planned and academic manner.

The ECPE assesses this skill because academic writing is essential for proficiency in English.

Time limit

You will be given thirty minutes to plan, write, and edit your essay.

Word count

Your ECPE essay should be a page and a half long in hand writing. This is usually around 450 to 600 words.

Question types

ECPE essay questions can be classified into two general groups.

The first type of essay question includes a thought-provoking statement on a topic and a question asking you to explain the advantages and disadvantages of the topic.

The type 2 essay will ask for your opinion on a topic and tell you to provide reasons to support your opinion.

Here is an example of a type 1 essay question:

Question: The only power any government has is the power to crack down on criminals. However, illegal activity should be overlooked when doing so brings benefits to society at large. What are the advantages and disadvantages to society of overlooking lesser crimes?

Here is an example of a type 2 essay question:

Question: Most Americans have access to computers and cell phones on a daily basis, making email and text messaging extremely popular. While some people argue that email and texting are now the most convenient forms of personal communication, others believe that electronic communication technology is often used inappropriately. Do you think that using digital communication is positive or negative? Give reasons and examples to support your viewpoint.

ECPE Essay Scoring

Your ECPE essay will be given a score from 1 to 5 in three different areas, for a total possible score of 15. The three following areas of your essay will be assessed:

1. **RHETORIC**

    Relevance – This means that your essay should answer the question that has been posed. You will need to express your main idea in a clear way in the introduction of the essay.

    The examiner assesses this aspect of your essay by searching for a thesis statement in the first paragraph of your essay.

    Development – It is extremely important to develop the main idea of your essay and maintain your point of view throughout your writing. Your essay should include examples and explanations that illustrate and support your viewpoint. Remember that if your essay topic presents a contentious issue, you should take a stance on the issue.

    Details and complexity – Your essay should demonstrate unity and coherence among the examples that you use to support your argument. Students sometimes worry about the point of view that they decide to take. However, you will not be assessed on your opinions themselves, but rather on how well you have expressed, organized, and supported them.

    Connection of ideas – Your essay should be divided into paragraphs, which have been set out in an organized manner. Each body paragraph should contain a point that supports your main idea. You should also include a conclusion that sums up the essay. The examiner looks for logical paragraph divisions, as well as for linking words and phrases that indicate a new paragraph is beginning.

2. **GRAMMAR AND SYNTAX**

    Accuracy of sentence construction – The examiner will look for a variety of sentence patterns. The examiner searches for linking words and phrases that signal that examples or reasons are being provided in the essay. These linking words and phrases include the following: such as, for example, for this reason, because of.

Range of construction – You should write long and developed sentences that demonstrate a variety of sentence patterns. You should avoid repeatedly beginning your sentences in the same way, such as "I think that."

Errors and control – Your essay should be grammatically accurate and punctuated correctly. Your spelling should also be correct.

The examiner will expect advanced grammar and correct spelling.

3. **VOCABULARY**

The examiner will check your vocabulary level because, generally speaking, using an advanced level of academic vocabulary demonstrates that your English skills are more advanced.

Range – The examiner will consider how advanced your vocabulary is.

Relevance and appropriateness – The examiner will evaluate whether your word choice and tone are appropriate to the question.

Be sure that you use academic vocabulary from the academic word list later in this book.

How to Avoid Common ECPE Essay Errors and Raise Your Score

In the previous section, we talked about the characteristics of a well-written ECPE essay. However, you may also wonder which aspects of an essay would be scored poorly by the ECPE examiner.

These errors most commonly cause students to receive a low ECPE essay score:

1. The essay fails to express a clear point of view or provides a viewpoint that is not logically supported.

    Tip: You can avoid this error by giving a clear thesis statement in the first paragraph of your essay.

2. The essay is written in a tone and style that is not suitable for an academic audience.

    Tip: Achieving the correct tone and style means that you need to avoid using informal or conversational expressions in your writing. Examples of informal language include words like "awesome" or "guy."

3. The reasons or examples provided in the essay are not relevant because they do not support the student's main point.

    Tip: Be sure that your reasons and examples are closely related to your main idea and to the essay topic. For instance, if you are asked whether art programs should be supported in schools, and then go on to talk about physical education programs because you believe they are similar to art programs, your reasoning would be flawed.

4. The essay is disorganized and therefore difficult to read and score.

    Tip: You can avoid this error by brainstorming your ideas and planning your essay before you begin writing.

5. The essay contains errors in sentence construction or contains only simple or repetitive sentence structures.

    Tip: Try to avoid writing every sentence of your essay in the subject-verb-object sentence pattern. In order to avoid this shortcoming, you can begin sentences with words and phrases like "although" or "because of this."

6. The essay does not demonstrate an advanced vocabulary level.

   Tip: Be sure that you give persuasive reasons and examples to state and support your position. Ensure that you have used academic vocabulary to express your ideas.

7. The essay contains errors in spelling, grammar, and punctuation.

   Tip: If you have weaknesses in these areas, you should study the "Using Correct Grammar and Punctuation" section at the end of this study guide.

ECPE Essay Structure

Assertion-Argument-Counterargument-Synthesis-Conclusion

The components of a well-written ECPE essay are:

- Assertion
- Argument
- Counterargument
- Synthesis
- Conclusion

In this unit, we give definitions and explanations for the above concepts, discussing each one of these components in turn.

In the next unit, we discuss alternative ways to organize these components in your ECPE essay, depending upon the argument you decide to put forward.

Formulating Your Assertion

In general, an assertion is a statement of your point of view on a particular problem or topic. In your essay, you should normally make your assertion in the first paragraph. Your assertion should be a clear statement that responds to the specific point raised in the essay question.

For instance, consider this essay question:

> *Many people believe that countries that are heavily reliant upon motorized vehicles for transport would do well to establish governmental measures to promote the practice of using non-motorized vehicles. What are the advantages and disadvantages of regulating the use of non-motorized vehicles?*

You will notice that the essay question already contains an assertion, so you need to think about the pros and cons of the situation before formulating your own assertion.

You can formulate your assertion by following these steps:

1. What are the advantages of the topic under discussion? In this case, the advantages of non-motorized transport include, among other things, the reduction of pollution, as well as health benefits to the general population (because people will walk and cycle more frequently).

2. Now think about the potential disadvantages. The general public often complain of government intervention in their lives and over-regulation of behaviors that should be left to common sense.

3. Finally, form your assertion for paragraph 1. Your assertion should indicate that you have an awareness that there is contention surrounding your position.

Remember that the first sentence of your ECPE essay needs to introduce your topic in a general way. You should put your assertion after the introductory sentence.

So, a possible first paragraph for the above essay topic is as follows:

There is a constant question in society nowadays about the environmental and health risks caused by the use of motorized vehicles. In spite of public complaints about the excessive involvement of the government in our private lives, it is irrefutable that increasing regulatory measures by a certain amount would bring about benefits to society.

You can also add a thesis statement at the end of your introductory paragraph. A thesis statement indicates how your essay is organized and gives a preview of the position you are going to take on the topic. Thesis statements often begin with the phrases "This essay will discuss…" or "I will show that…."

In reality, though, a thesis statement is not always necessary for ECPE essays because you will have already indicated your position in your assertion sentence.

In the above example, the writer's position is that his or her proposal "would bring about benefits to society."

If you prefer to add a thesis statement to your ECPE essay, the first paragraph would look something like this:

> There is a constant question in society nowadays about the environmental and health risks caused by the use of motorized vehicles. In spite of public complaints about the excessive involvement of the government in our private lives, it is irrefutable that increasing regulatory measures by a certain amount would bring about benefits to society. This essay will discuss the supporters and detractors to governmental involvement in the realm of traffic control, before describing two measures that the government might take to address the issue.

So, in the paragraph above, the thesis statement is as follows:

> This essay will discuss the supporters and detractors to governmental involvement in the realm of traffic control, before describing two measures that the government might take to address the issue.

Before moving on to the next section, we must point out that you will need to make other assertions in your essay when you provide your supporting points. However, remember that your essay will be the most effective when you begin with a strong statement of your overall position in your assertion in the first paragraph.

Supporting and Sustaining Your Argument

In an essay, an argument is when you provide reasons and examples to support your position.

- Remember that the essence of a good argument is that it gives persuasive and convincing reasons and examples to support the development of the essay.
- In other words, you need to provide valid points that support your opinion.
- You can express your argument effectively by using the argumentative language provided in one of the subsequent units in this book.
- In the subsequent units, we will also show you how to use other words and phrases to express and strengthen assertions that you make in your argument.
- You should note that, at times, you may need to limit your assertions, depending upon the strength and validity of the opposing views.

Now let's look again at our example essay topic and the first paragraph to the essay:

Many people believe that countries that are heavily reliant upon motorized vehicles for transport would do well to establish governmental measures to promote the practice of using non-motorized vehicles. What are the advantages and disadvantages of regulating the use of non-motorized vehicles?

There is a constant question in society nowadays about the environmental and health risks caused by the use of motorized vehicles. In spite of public complaints about the excessive involvement of the government in our private lives, it is irrefutable that increasing regulatory measures by a certain amount would bring about benefits to society.

Because the assertion in the above paragraph is that "increasing regulatory measures by a certain amount would bring about benefits to society," your argument should continue in the second paragraph by giving reasons for and examples of the benefits that will be derived from such a measure.

By continuing with a discussion of benefits, you ensure that your argument has a good flow.

Achieving good flow will make your essay more persuasive and will also make it easier to read.

Now recall the advantages that we came up with when preparing our primary assertion. The advantages to governmental involvement in traffic control were:

1. The reduction of pollution
2. Health benefits to the general population because of more frequent walking and cycling.

Then decide which one of these advantages has more strength, in your opinion. Remember that an argument will be stronger when you can give evidence or examples to support it.

In this essay, we will use the health argument in the second paragraph, giving evidence from Denmark.

Here is a possible second paragraph for our essay topic:

> There is no doubt that countries using non-motorized transport as a norm have a better level of health in the general population. In Denmark, where most people cycle to work, it is reported that levels of heart disease and stroke are far lower than they are in other countries.

You can see that by backing up your assertion with a concrete example, like the one about Denmark above, you give your assertion more strength.

Acknowledging and Refuting the Counterargument

The counterargument is the viewpoint that is against your opinion.

- Just as with your argument, you will need to give reasons and examples to support the counterargument to demonstrate that you understand your opponent's concerns.
- If you do not do this, your essay might appear too simple or limited.
- When you express the counterargument, it will be beneficial to use argumentative language.
- Using argumentative language will show that you understand the strength of your opponent's position, while distancing your opinion from the opposing viewpoint.

For your convenience, we provide the second paragraph of the essay again below:

> There is no doubt that countries using non-motorized transport as a norm have a better level of health in the general population. In Denmark, where most people cycle to work, it is reported that levels of heart disease and stroke are far lower than they are in other countries.

Notice that up to this point the second paragraph has spoken in support of your assertion, which is that "increasing regulatory measures by a certain amount would bring about benefits to society." Now we have to address the drawbacks to your assertion.

Recall the disadvantage that we mentioned when preparing our primary assertion.

The disadvantages to governmental involvement in traffic control are:

1. The general public often complain of government intervention in their lives.
2. The government over-regulates day-to-day behaviors that should be left to common sense.

Bearing in mind these disadvantages, here is one possible way to continue the second paragraph of our essay:

> In spite of the health benefits, some would argue that cycling as a means of transport must be a matter left to personal choice. We constantly hear objections from the public about policies that cause unnecessary governmental intervention and bureaucracy in our lives. They claim the choice of whether or not to use an environmentally-friendly form of transport should be a matter of individual conscience. But we only have to consider the rising levels of environmental damage around the world to understand that personal choice and individual conscience as a means to improving the environment have, in fact, been ineffective thus far.

Notice the argumentative language ("some would argue that…" and "They claim") in the first and third sentences. These phrases help to identify this response as a viewpoint that opposes your own.

You also place a distance between your own view and the opposite viewpoint because you clearly identify the other side as "some" and "they."

In addition to using argumentative language, you will normally come to some sort of resolution after you state the opposing viewpoint. Notice how the opposing viewpoint in the second paragraph is resolved by the final sentence:

> But we only have to consider the rising levels of environmental damage around the world to understand that personal choice and individual conscience as a means to improving the environment have, in fact, been ineffective thus far.

Such a resolution provides a good transition into the next paragraph of your essay and also serves to improve the flow of your writing.

Extending and Elaborating Your Argument

To achieve a high score, it normally will not be sufficient to give only one argument in your essay.

On a practical level, your essay should be 450 words at a minimum, and it would be difficult to achieve that amount without giving a second argument.

More significantly, if you do not give a second argument and elaborate on it, your essay may appear underdeveloped.

So, the next step is to think about how to extend your argument in paragraph 3.

In the final part of paragraph 2, we talked about our opponent's view: there should be an element of personal choice in deciding to use alternative forms of transport. In essence, this belief in personal choice is the cornerstone of our opponent's view.

So, in the next part of the essay, we need to think about how to advance our argument further and undermine our opponent. In our sample essay on traffic control, we can undermine our opponent by finding flaws with the aspect of personal choice.

Think about countries where inhabitants do not always have the luxury of personally choosing to use an automobile, such as in the Far East. Then cite examples of countries where personal choice has led to excessive gasoline consumption, such as in the United States.

Having planned our line of reasoning, here is a possible second argument for the third paragraph for our essay:

> One only needs to look at certain remote villages in the Far East, where the aspect of personal choice has been removed because motorized vehicles cannot be afforded. In doing so, one can see that levels of air pollution and other forms of environmental contamination are far less in these villages than in so-called "developed" countries. Consider the converse case, for instance, in the United States, where a heavy reliance on motor vehicles has resulted in this country being one of the largest emitters of greenhouse gases in the world.

Note that it is not strictly necessary to attempt to refute your second argument by providing another counterargument. In fact, sometimes giving another counterargument at this point would weaken your position.

In the example above, we provide the second argument about villages in the Far East. We then elaborate and strengthen that argument by citing a further example in the United States.

We also elaborate rather than counter-argue at this point because the idea of rising pollution levels was already mentioned in paragraph 2.

While this sample essay has two main arguments, please note that it is likely that you may even need to have a third argument in your essay in order to elaborate your ideas fully.

Synthesizing the Viewpoints

In your ECPE essay, your synthesis is where you continue to acknowledge the opposing viewpoint, while showing that your assertions and arguments hold more weight than your opponent's.

- A synthesis can simply consist of a strong reiteration of your assertion and the reasons why it is still true.
- A synthesis can sometimes involve arriving at some sort of compromise between the opposing viewpoints.
- If you are going to offer a compromise, you need to state the specific conditions of it in your synthesis.

The following synthesis for our example essay includes a proposed compromise:

Therefore, it is evident that a compromise needs to be reached in order to balance the limitations on personal freedom that can result from imposing governmental control over the issue, on the one hand, while addressing the very exigent concerns of cleaning up the world's environment and promoting healthy habits amongst its inhabitants, on the other. After all, it is often stated that personal freedom of choice is the cornerstone of any democratic society.

Notice that the synthesis above uses the key words "compromise" and "in order to balance" to indicate clearly that a compromise is being proposed.

The balancing of opposing viewpoints is also signaled by the phrases "on the one hand" and "on the other."

Writing Your Conclusion

The conclusion to your ECPE essay consists of your final comments, which need to indicate the proposition that you are putting forward in response to the issue at hand.

In other words, your conclusion needs to state the specific conditions of the outcome that you are proposing.

- You may need to re-state your position in your conclusion.

- Your conclusion is normally placed directly after the synthesis.

- The conclusion is often in the same paragraph as your synthesis.

- You may offer solutions to the problem in your conclusion.

The following conclusion for our example essay puts forward two possible solutions:

> Perhaps the best solution to the issue at hand is to have the government provide certain incentives to those who decide not to use motorized vehicles. For instance, the government could offer rebates or subsidies on bicycle purchases. Another possible course of action would be to introduce certain governmental controls, but to establish those controls within very clear limits. Alternating car use by vehicle registration number has been an effective solution in certain countries. Under this scheme, car owners with odd-numbered registrations can use their vehicles on certain days of the week, while owners of vehicles with registrations

ending in an even number are permitted to use their vehicles only on the other days. Violating this policy would result in fines or other sanctions.

To sum up, one thing is clear: whether by positive reinforcement, as in the first example, or by negative reinforcement as in the second, both remedies take into account the pressing concern of the state of the global environment, as well as protecting the need of the population for both personal health and individual freedom.

In the example above, two possible courses of action are put forward: one is an incentive plan, and the other is a plan involving fines and sanctions.

Notice how both courses of action are described precisely and with sufficient detail.

Closing your essay in this way leaves a positive impact on the person who is reading and evaluating it.

Sample Essay 1

We reproduce the entire example essay in full here so that you can see how the parts relate to each other and how it achieves a good line of argument.

> *Many people believe that countries that are heavily reliant upon motorized vehicles for transport would do well to establish governmental measures to promote the practice of using non-motorized vehicles. What are the advantages and disadvantages of regulating the use of non-motorized vehicles?*

There is a constant question in society nowadays about the environmental and health risks caused by the use of motorized vehicles. In spite of public complaints about the excessive involvement of the government in our private lives, it is irrefutable that increasing regulatory measures by a certain amount would bring about benefits to society. This essay will discuss the supporters and detractors to governmental involvement in the realm of traffic control, before describing two measures that the government might take to address the issue.

There is no doubt that countries using non-motorized transport as a norm have a better level of health in the general population. In Denmark, where most people cycle to work, it is reported that levels of heart disease and stroke are far lower than they are in other countries. In spite of the health benefits, some would argue that cycling as a means of transport must be a matter left to personal choice. We constantly hear objections from the public about policies that cause unnecessary governmental intervention and bureaucracy in our lives. They claim the choice of whether or not to use an environmentally-friendly form of transport should be a matter of individual conscience. But we only have to consider the rising levels of environmental damage around the world to understand that personal choice and individual conscience as a means to improving the environment have, in fact, been ineffective thus far.

One only needs to look at certain remote villages in the Far East, where the aspect of personal choice has been removed because motorized vehicles cannot be afforded. In doing so, one can see that levels of air pollution and other forms of environmental contamination are far less in these villages than in so-called "developed" countries. Consider the converse case, for instance, in the United States, where a heavy reliance on motor vehicles has resulted in this country being one of the largest emitters of greenhouse gases in the world.

Therefore, it is evident that a compromise needs to be reached in order to balance the limitations on personal freedom that can result from imposing governmental control over the issue, on the one hand, while addressing the very exigent concerns of cleaning up the world's environment and promoting healthy habits amongst its inhabitants, on the other. After all, it is often stated that personal freedom of choice is the cornerstone of any democratic society. Perhaps the best solution to the issue at hand is to have the government provide certain incentives to those who decide not to use motorized vehicles. For instance, the government could offer rebates or subsidies on bicycle purchases. Another possible course of action would be to introduce certain governmental controls, but to establish those controls within very clear limits. Alternating car use by vehicle registration number has been an effective solution in certain countries. Under this scheme, car owners with odd-numbered registrations can use their vehicles on certain days of the week, while owners of vehicles with registrations ending in an even number are permitted to use their vehicles only on the other days. Violating this policy would result in fines or other sanctions. To sum up, one thing is clear: whether by positive reinforcement, as in the first example, or by negative reinforcement as in the second, both remedies take into account the pressing concern of the state of the global environment, as well as protecting the need of the population for both personal health and individual freedom.

ECPE Essays:
The Key Points Summed Up

So, to sum up our discussion, here's a brief list of key points to bear in mind when writing your ECPE essay.

How to argue your point:

- Answer the question with a strong assertion
- Provide arguments that you support with reasons and examples
- Address arguments which contradict your own opinion
- Provide a synthesis and conclusion

Organizing Your ECPE Essay

We know that an ECPE essay contains the following elements: Assertion, Argument, Counterargument, Synthesis, and Conclusion. However, you may have some doubt regarding how these individual elements should be organized. While the organization of your essay can vary depending on your writing skill and technique, as well as the essay theme, we believe that there are two particular organization schemes which are especially effective for the ECPE essay. They are as follows:

Scheme 1

- Assertion
- Argument 1
- Counterargument
- Argument 2
- Elaboration
- Synthesis
- Conclusion

A scheme 1 organizational style was used in the sample essay on non-motorized vehicles given in the previous section. When considering the amount and strength of existing counterarguments, however, it may be more beneficial in some cases to use the scheme 2 organizational style.

Scheme 2

- Assertion
- Argument 1
- Counterargument 1
- Argument 2
- Counterargument 2
- Synthesis
- Conclusion

As stated previously, it may be necessary in some cases to give more than two arguments and counterarguments; the above guidelines are offered by way of general advice on structure and organization.

We provide an example of an essay written using scheme 2 in sample essay 2 in this publication, which is on the theme of tourism.

What is "Argumentative Language"?

In previous units in this publication, we have touched on the notion of "argumentative language."

"Argumentative language" means the words and phrases that you can use to introduce your own assertions and elaborations on those assertions.

You can also use argumentative language to introduce and distance yourself from opposing viewpoints.

Let's look at the argumentative language used in paragraph 1 of sample essay 1:

<u>There is a constant question</u> in society nowadays about the environmental and health risks caused by the use of motorized vehicles. In spite of public complaints about the excessive involvement of the government in our private lives, <u>it is irrefutable that</u> increasing regulatory measures <u>by a certain amount</u> would bring about benefits to society. This essay will discuss the supporters and detractors to this assertion, before describing two measures that the government might take to address the issue.

Exercise: Now look at the reminder of sample essay 1 and underline the argumentative language. Please do not underline linking words (for example, because, in spite of, etc.) because we will analyze those in a later unit.

The answer is provided on the pages immediately following this exercise.

There is no doubt that countries using non-motorized transport as a norm have a better level of health in the general population. In Denmark, where most people cycle to work, it is reported that levels of heart disease and stroke are far lower than they are in other countries. In spite of the health benefits, some would argue that cycling as a means of transport must be a matter left to personal choice. We constantly hear objections from the public about policies that cause unnecessary governmental intervention and bureaucracy in our lives. They claim the choice of whether or not to use an environmentally-friendly form of transport should be a matter of individual conscience. But we only have to consider the rising levels of environmental damage around the world to understand that personal choice and individual conscience as a means to improving the environment have, in fact, been ineffective thus far.

One only needs to look at certain remote villages in the Far East, where the aspect of personal choice has been removed because motorized vehicles cannot be afforded. In doing so, one can see that levels of air pollution and other forms of environmental contamination are far less in these villages than in so-called "developed" countries. Consider the converse case, for instance, in the United States, where a heavy reliance on motor vehicles has resulted in this country being one of the largest emitters of greenhouse gases in the world.

Therefore, it is evident that a compromise needs to be reached in order to balance the limitations on personal freedom that can result from imposing governmental control over the issue, on the one hand, while addressing the very exigent concerns of cleaning up the world's environment and promoting healthy habits amongst its inhabitants, on the other. After all, it is often stated that personal freedom of choice is the cornerstone of any democratic society. Perhaps the best solution to the issue at hand is to have the government provide certain incentives to those who decide not to use motorized vehicles. For instance, the government could offer rebates or subsidies on bicycle purchases.

Another possible course of action would be to introduce certain governmental controls, but to establish those controls within very clear limits. Alternating car use by vehicle registration number has been an effective solution in certain countries. Under this scheme, car owners with odd-numbered registrations can use their vehicles on certain days of the week, while owners of vehicles with registrations ending in an even number are only permitted to use their vehicles on the other days. Violating this policy would result in fines or other sanctions. To sum up, one thing is clear: whether by positive reinforcement, as in the first example, or by negative reinforcement as in the second, both remedies take into account the pressing concern of the state of the global environment, as well as protecting the need of the population for both personal health and individual freedom.

Answer to Argumentative Language Exercise

There is no doubt that countries using non-motorized transport as a norm have a better level of health in the general population. In Denmark, where most people cycle to work, it is reported that levels of heart disease and stroke are far lower than they are in other countries. In spite of the health benefits, some would argue that cycling as a means of transport must be a matter left to personal choice. We constantly hear objections from the public about policies that cause unnecessary governmental intervention and bureaucracy in our lives. They claim, the choice of whether or not to use an environmentally-friendly form of transport should be a matter of individual conscience. But we only have to consider the rising levels of environmental damage around the world to understand that personal choice and individual conscience as a means to improving the environment have, in fact, been ineffective thus far.

One only needs to look at certain remote villages in the Far East, where the aspect of personal choice has been removed because motorized vehicles cannot be afforded. In doing so, one can see that levels of air pollution and other forms of environmental contamination are far less in these villages than in so-called "developed" countries. Consider the converse case, for instance, in the United States, a heavy reliance on motor vehicles has resulted in this country being one of the largest emitters of greenhouse gases in the world.

Therefore, it is evident that a compromise needs to be reached in order to balance the limitations on personal freedom that can result from imposing governmental control over the issue, on the one hand, while addressing the very exigent concerns of cleaning up the world's environment and promoting healthy habits amongst its inhabitants, on the other. After all, it is often stated that personal freedom of choice is the cornerstone of any democratic society. Perhaps the best solution to the issue at hand is to have the government provide certain incentives to those who decide not to use motorized vehicles. For instance, the government could offer rebates or subsidies on bicycle purchases.

Another possible course of action would be to introduce certain governmental controls, but to establish those controls within very clear limits. Alternating car use by vehicle registration number has been an effective solution in certain countries. Under this scheme, car owners with odd-numbered registrations can use their vehicles on certain days of the week, while owners of vehicles with registrations ending in an even number are only permitted to use their vehicles on the other days. Violating this policy would result in fines or other sanctions. To sum up, one thing is clear: whether by positive reinforcement, as in the first example, or by negative reinforcement as in the second, both remedies take into account the pressing concern of the state of the global environment, as well as protecting the need of the population for both personal health and individual freedom.

Please notice that, depending on how you structure your essay, some of the phrases above may be used to support your assertions, and alternatively the same phrases could be used to distance yourself from your opponent's claims. It's a matter of how cautious and diplomatic you want to be.

If the above exercise was a struggle for you, we recommend that you make a list of the above phrases and memorize them to use some in your essay on the day of your actual ECPE exam.

Using Linking Words and Phrases Effectively in Your ECPE Essay

The effective use of linking words and phrases will make your ECPE essay more organized and easier to read.

Unfortunately, problems can occur with punctuation and word placement when using linking words and phrases. In order to make the best impact with your ECPE essay, you should be sure to observe the conventions of correct grammar and punctuation.

Linking words and phrases fall into three categories. Please read the following rules for word placement and punctuation for each category:

1) The first category of linking words and phrases is the **sentence linker.** Sentence linkers are usually placed at the beginning of a sentence and are followed by a comma.

Look at this example of using a sentence linker at the start of the sentence:

However, you should still study hard.

For emphasis, you can use sentence linkers in the middle of a sentence. If you do so, be sure that you put commas both before and after the sentence linker. Now look at this example to see how a sentence linker is used in the middle of a sentence:

You should, *however*, still study hard.

2) The second category of linking words and phrases is the **phrase linker**. Phrase linkers must be followed by a noun or noun phrase (a phrase does not contain a verb).

Phrase linkers should not be followed by a clause (a clause contains at least one verb).

Now look at this phrase linker example:

He passed the exam *because of* his preparation.

"His preparation" is a noun phrase. In other words, it does not contain a verb. Remember that verbs are words that show action.

3) The third category of linking words and phrases is the **subordinator**. Subordinators must be followed by a clause. Subordinators should not be followed by a phrase.

Again, remember that clauses must contain at least one verb.

Here is a subordinator example:

Although he worked hard, he failed to make his business successful.

"Although" is a subordinator. In the above example sentence "he worked hard" is a clause. The verb is "worked."

On the following pages, we provide a list of the most common linking words and phrases, grouped according to their category. Note which ones are sentence linkers, which ones are phrase linkers, and which ones are subordinators. You will use these words and phrases in the exercise that follows the list.

Linking Words and Phrases:

<u>Sentence linkers for giving additional information</u>

further

furthermore

apart from this

what is more

in addition

additionally

in the same way

moreover

<u>Sentence linkers for giving examples</u>

for example

for instance

firstly / first of all

in this case

in particular

mainly

more precisely

namely

in brief / in short

in essence

<u>Phrase linkers for giving specific information</u>

particularly

especially

specifically

<u>Sentence linkers for stating the obvious</u>

obviously

clearly

naturally

of course

surely

after all

<u>Phrase linkers for giving generalizations</u>

in general

on the whole

as a rule

for the most part

generally speaking

in most cases

Sentence linkers for stating causes and effects

thus

accordingly

hence

therefore

in that case

under those circumstances

as a result

for this reason

as a consequence

consequently

in effect

Phrase linkers for stating causes and effects

because of

due to

Subordinators for stating causes and effects

because

since

Sentence linkers for showing contrast

on the other hand

on the contrary

alternatively

rather

otherwise

Phrase linker for showing contrast

in contrast to

Sentence linkers for showing similarity

similarly

in the same way

likewise

Phrase linker for showing similarity

just like

Sentence linkers for paraphrasing or restating

in other words

that is to say

that is

Subordinators	Sentence linkers for concession or unexpected results
after	however
although	nevertheless
as	still
before	yet
even though	meanwhile
if	**Phrase linkers for concession or unexpected results**
since	despite
so / so that	in spite of
that	but rather
unless	**Sentence linkers for giving conclusions**
until	finally
when	to conclude
while	lastly
whereas	in conclusion
not only . . . but also	
as well as	
besides	

Exercise: Read the essay that follows and place the linking words or phrases provided below into the correct gaps. When you have finished, compare your answers to those in sample essay 2.

for instance / hence / although / because / because of / not only / but also / yet / further / first of all / even though / nevertheless / in addition / however

The effect of tourism on a country's economy can be astounding. Yet, the expansion of tourism also brings with it certain dangers. Do you think that tourism brings more harm than good to the poorer countries of the world? Give reasons and examples to support your viewpoint.

Cheaper flights are making it more and more affordable and convenient for people around the world to travel to other countries. In the US alone, there has been a recent proliferation in low-cost and budget airlines, which has made it easier for the average family to afford a vacation to some "exotic" destination. _____ , in many cases, "exotic" may mean one of the less economically well-off countries of the world. Sometimes having less infrastructure and being removed from the hustle and bustle of the vacationer's normal life, these destinations are selected because they are seen as holding a restorative balm to modern life's daily stresses. _____ such trips may be beneficial for the traveler, the negative effects of the increasing throngs of tourists on the poorer countries of the world should give us reason to take pause _____ it is clear that there are problems associated with the expanding global tourism industry.

Apart from the obvious environmental damage that tourism causes, _____ , we must consider increasing crime rates. Some local residents might see tourists as easy prey because, _____ are they in unfamiliar territory and therefore less able to take care of themselves, _____ because they carry visible items of wealth such as jewelry and electronic equipment, which can be readily resold for a quick profit. _____, vacationers might argue in response to this claim that they know how to protect themselves, so there is no danger. Some might even claim that they leave all valuables home when traveling abroad. _____, such arguments focus merely on theft, without taking in account other crimes. _____, some people will knowingly purchase illegal copies of films from a vendor abroad that sells pirated copies of digital goods. Believing that the authorities turn a blind eye to such "soft" crimes, normally law-abiding tourists behave in this way because they realize that they can do so with impunity. Consider the even more extreme case of tourists who go abroad to take advantage of that country's lack of enforcement of recreational drug use or prostitution. _____ recreational drugs and prostitution are illegal in certain of these countries, some tourists again believe that they can justify their actions merely because of the fact that they will escape punishment. _____, these tourists fail to consider that these crimes are not enforced because of the country's economic conditions in the first place, and that by participating in these crimes, they are exacerbating and perpetuating crime even further in the host country.

_____, another major problem is healthcare. With greater mobility comes greater danger of spreading contagious diseases. On a local level, tourists' illnesses, accidents, and injuries place a strain on local healthcare systems and in extreme cases can threaten the lives of the local people who are unaccustomed to certain strains of diseases. Vacationers might claim that they would not consider traveling when they are under the weather. _____, others might argue that they never travel without getting a medical insurance policy for their trips. Nevertheless, the flaws in these arguments can easily be revealed: people can carry strains of bacteria-causing illnesses without feeling unwell, and regardless of whether one is in possession of a medical insurance policy or not, he or she might require a stay in a local hospital _____ the illness or injury, thereby putting further strain on local resources.

These are just two reasons why tourism can do more harm than good. These phenomena suggest that one should devote careful awareness to his or her selection of a tourist destination by taking into consideration the effects of one's proposed trip on the host country. All in all, it might appear that "voluntourism" will become more popular in the future if the general public takes the needs of the host country into account when deciding where to go on vacation.

Sample Essay 2

It can be argued that tourism brings more harm than good to the poorer countries of the world. Do you think that the benefits of the tourist industry are greater than the harm it causes? Give reasons to support your opinion.

Cheaper flights are making it more and more affordable and convenient for people around the world to travel to other countries. In the US alone, there has been a recent proliferation in low-cost and budget airlines, which has made it easier for the average family to afford a vacation to some "exotic" destination. However, in many cases, "exotic" may mean one of the less economically well-off countries of the world. Sometimes having less infrastructure and being removed from the hustle and bustle of the vacationer's normal life, these destinations are selected because they are seen as holding a restorative balm to modern life's daily stresses. Although such trips may be beneficial for the traveler, the negative effects of the increasing throngs of tourists on the poorer countries of the world should give us reason to take pause because it is clear that there are problems associated with the expanding global tourism industry.

Apart from the obvious environmental damage that tourism causes, first of all, we must consider increasing crime rates. Some local residents might see tourists as easy prey because, not only are they in unfamiliar territory and therefore less able to take care of themselves, but also because they carry visible items of wealth such as jewelry and electronic equipment, which can be readily resold for a quick profit. Nevertheless, vacationers might argue in response to this claim that they know how to protect themselves, so there is no danger. Some might even claim that they leave all valuables home when traveling abroad. Yet, such arguments focus merely on theft, without taking in account other crimes. For instance, some people will knowingly purchase illegal copies of films from a vendor abroad that sells pirated copies of digital goods. Believing that the authorities turn a blind eye to such "soft" crimes, normally law-abiding tourists behave in this way because they realize that they can do so with impunity. Consider the even more extreme case of tourists who go abroad to take advantage of that country's lack of enforcement of recreational drug use or prostitution. Even though recreational drugs and prostitution are illegal in certain of these countries, some tourists again believe that they can justify their actions merely because of the fact that they will escape punishment. Hence, these tourists fail to consider that these crimes are not enforced because of the country's economic conditions in the first place, and that by participating in these crimes, they are exacerbating and perpetuating crime even further in the host country.

In addition, another major problem is healthcare. With greater mobility comes greater danger of spreading contagious diseases. On a local level, tourists' illnesses, accidents, and injuries place a strain on local healthcare systems and in extreme cases can threaten the lives of the local people who are unaccustomed to certain strains of diseases. Vacationers might claim that they would not consider traveling when they are under the weather. <u>Further</u>, others might argue that they never travel without getting a medical insurance policy for their trips. Nevertheless, the flaws in these arguments can easily be revealed: people can carry strains of bacteria-causing illnesses without feeling unwell, and regardless of whether one is in possession of a medical insurance policy or not, he or she might require a stay in a local hospital <u>because of</u> the illness or injury, thereby putting further strain on local resources.

These are just two reasons why tourism can do more harm than good. These phenomena suggest that one should devote careful awareness to his or her selection of a tourist destination by taking into consideration the effects of one's proposed trip on the host country. All in all, it might appear that "voluntourism" will become more popular in the future if the general public takes the needs of the host country into account when deciding where to go on vacation.

Please note that you can interchange positions of the following words:

However / Nevertheless / Yet

Although / Even though

In addition / Further

Using Adjectives to Assert Your Opinion

Adjectives are words that are used to describe nouns. You should use adjectives in your ECPE essay to strengthen your assertions, as well as to weaken your opponent's claims.

- Remember that a noun can normally be classified as a person, place, or thing.
- For example, in the sentence "Science is a boring subject" the word "boring" is an adjective and the word "subject" is a thing.

Now look at these two sentences:

The present rate of global warming is a problem in the world today.

The present rate of global warming is an exigent problem in the world today.

The second sentence is much more persuasive than the first because it uses the adjective "exigent" to emphasize that the problem is extremely urgent or pressing.

Exercise*: Look at the following sentences and underline the adjectives that the writer uses to advance her assertions. Then make a mental note of these adjectives so that you can use them in your ECPE essay. The answers are provided on the following page.*

1) This nation's history is its greatest asset.

2) The landscape is an integral part of our identity.

3) Our heritage is fundamental to our culture.

4) Accepting change is a critical part of making decisions.

5) This decision is of paramount importance.

6) Historical buildings are a key part of our culture.

7) Clear policies on this issue are essential.

Answers to the Adjective Exercise

1) This nation's history is its <u>greatest</u> asset.

2) The landscape is an <u>integral</u> part of our identity.

3) Our heritage is <u>fundamental</u> to our culture.

4) Accepting change is a <u>critical</u> part of making decisions.

5) This decision is of <u>paramount</u> importance.

6) Historical buildings are a <u>key</u> part of our culture.

7) <u>Clear</u> policies on this issue are <u>essential</u>.

Using Modality to Argue Your Case

When we talk about "modality" in grammar, we are referring to the use of modal verbs in writing.

- Modal verbs include the following: can, could, may, must, ought to, shall, should, would, have to
- Modal verbs are extremely useful in ECPE essays because they can be used to help express your assertions and strengthen your examples.
- Modal verbs can also be used to limit the intensity of the opposing viewpoint.
- Remember that you can use modal verbs in either the affirmative or negative form.
- For example, "should" is the affirmative form, while "should not" is the negative form.

Exercise: Place the correct modal verb in the sentence below from the options provided at the end of each sentence. Notice that in some sentences, both options are correct. When both options are correct, please state which option strengthens the assertion the most. The answers are provided on the following page.

1) We _____ not hide our heritage. (should / have to)

2) We do not _____ look far to encounter this phenomenon. (have to / must)

3) We _____ not make that decision arbitrarily. (must / should)

4) We _____ work together to achieve this aim. (shall / could)

5) We _____ protect the environment. (would / ought to)

Answers to Modality Exercise

1) We _____ not hide our heritage. (should / have to)

   The correct answer is "should."

   In order to use "have to," the word order would be different: We do not have to hide our heritage.

2) We do not _____ look far to encounter this phenomenon. (have to / must)

   The correct answer is "have to." Must is incorrect grammatically.

3) We _____ not make that decision arbitrarily. (must / should)

   Both answers are correct. "Must" is stronger than "should" in this case because it is used to expresses a strong obligation, rather than a recommendation (as is the case of "should" in this sentence).

4) We _____ work together to achieve this aim. (shall / could)

   Both answers are correct. "Shall" is stronger than "could" because it expresses a future intention, rather than a mere possibility.

5) We _____ protect the environment. (would / ought to)

   The correct answer is "ought to." "Would" does not provide the correct sense to the sentence.

Using Qualifiers to Strengthen or Limit Your Assertions

"Qualify" means limit or modify, particularly to modify the meaning of a word or phrase. Qualifiers are words that can be used in your ECPE essay either to make your assertions sound more serious or to advance your own arguments.

- Qualifiers can also be used to acknowledge your opponent's viewpoints
- Qualifiers often include words that can be used as adverbs, such as: surely, fairly, evidently
- Adverbs often end with the letters –ly.

Exercise: *Imagine that you are writing an argumentative essay asserting that the government's economic policies and proposals are largely ineffectual. Please underline the qualifier in each sentence. Then state whether the qualifier is being used to support your own argument or to acknowledge your opponent's viewpoints.*

1) Admittedly, the government's plans have some redeeming features.

2) This economic policy has been rightly criticized.

3) There are certainly advantages to this economic proposal.

4) Equally there are arguments against the proposal.

5) However, policy and reality are often mutually exclusive.

Answers to the Qualifiers Exercise

1) <u>Admittedly</u>, the government's plans have some redeeming features.

   You will recall that your argument is that the government's economic policies and proposals are largely ineffectual. So, the qualifier in the sentence above is being used to acknowledge your opponent's viewpoints.

2) This economic policy has been <u>rightly</u> criticized.
   Used to advance your own argument

3) There are <u>certainly</u> advantages to this economic proposal.

   Used to acknowledge your opponent's viewpoints

4) <u>Equally</u> there are arguments against the proposal.

   Used to advance your own argument

5) However, policy and reality are often <u>mutually</u> exclusive.

   Used to advance your own argument

Using Verbs in the Argument and Counterargument

Verbs are words that show action. Practice how to use verbs to your advantage in your ECPE essay by completing the exercise below.

Exercise: *Sample essay 2 was an argumentative essay about whether tourism brings more harm than good to the poorer counties of the world. Some sentences from that essay are reproduced below. Look at the list of useful argumentative verbs and verb phrases on the page following the exercise. Then read the sentences below and underline all of the argumentative verb forms in each sentence. Note that you should not identify every verb, but only the argumentative ones. The answers to the exercises are given on the page following the verb list.*

1) Nevertheless, vacationers might argue in response to this claim that they know how to protect themselves, so there is no danger.

2) Some might even claim that they leave all valuables home when travelling abroad.

3) Yet, such arguments focus merely on theft, without taking in account other crimes.

4) Believing that the authorities turn a blind eye to such "soft" crimes, normally law-abiding tourists behave in this way because they realize that they can do so with impunity.

5) Consider the even more extreme case of tourists who go abroad to take advantage of that country's lack of enforcement of recreational drug use or prostitution.

6) Even though recreational drugs and prostitution are illegal in certain of these countries, some tourists again believe that they can justify their actions merely because of the fact that they will escape punishment.

7) Hence, these tourists fail to consider that these crimes are not enforced because of the country's economic conditions in the first place, and that by participating in these crimes, they are exacerbating and perpetuating crime even further in the host country.

Useful Verbs for the Argument and Counterargument

address	demonstrate
afford (meaning: provide)	deny
agree	disagree
approach	discern
argue	dispute
assert	emphasize
assume	enumerate
believe	exacerbate
challenge	hasten
claim	hold / hold the view
coerce	imply
comment	infer
conclude	influence
consider	maintain
concede	perpetrate
contend	perpetuate
contradict	persuade
convince	peruse

point out	report
ponder	repudiate
propose	reveal
protect	say
qualify	state
query	suggest
question	sum up
realize	stipulate
recognize	take heed
recommend	take into account
refute	view
reject	value
remark	warn

Answers to the Verb Exercise

1) Nevertheless, vacationers might <u>argue</u> in response to this claim that they know how to protect themselves, so there is no danger.

2) Some might even <u>claim</u> that they leave all valuables home when travelling abroad.

3) Yet, such arguments focus merely on theft, without <u>taking in account</u> other crimes.

4) <u>Believing</u> that the authorities turn a blind eye to such "soft" crimes, normally law-abiding tourists behave in this way because they <u>realize</u> that they can do so with impunity.

5) <u>Consider</u> the even more extreme case of tourists who go abroad to take advantage of that country's lack of enforcement of recreational drug use or prostitution.

6) Even though recreational drugs and prostitution are illegal in certain of these countries, some tourists again <u>believe</u> that they can justify their actions merely because of the fact that they will escape punishment.

7) Hence, these tourists fail to <u>consider</u> that these crimes are not enforced because of the country's economic conditions in the first place, and that by participating in these crimes, they are <u>exacerbating</u> and <u>perpetuating</u> crime even further in the host country.

ECPE Practice Test 3

Now that you have completed the review exercises, you should attempt the following practice test. Remember to allow 30 minutes to take each test. A model response is provided in the next section.

Answer one of the following questions:

1) Advertising is everywhere in our daily lives, from our computer screens to public areas. Yet, some people think that advertising serves only to manipulate the public, rather than to provide information. Do you think that the advantages of advertising outweigh the disadvantages?

2) Some people believe that all immigrants wishing to reside permanently in the United States should be required to show evidence of English language proficiency. Do you agree? Give reasons to support your opinion.

Sample Essay 3

This essay is in response to essay question 1 on the previous page. A detailed analysis of the essay is provided after the written essay response.

Advertising is a powerful force in today's materialistic, status-conscious society. Consumers are bombarded with advertising at every turn, from advertisements on television and radio, to outdoor advertising on electronic signs and even on buses. The abundance of advertising that confronts a person from one day to the next thus leaves one to wonder: How much of this advertising is really useful or necessary? This essay will reveal that while the majority of advertising serves only to drive mindless consumerism, a certain form of advertising does, in fact, serve a useful purpose.

Most advertising that we see nowadays, especially that on television, is the attempt of large companies to persuade the general public to buy products that they do not need and may not ultimately want. In other words, advertisements do not truly exist to give product information to consumers, but rather to coerce them mentally into buying the product in question. Further, I would argue that this phenomenon has larger economic repercussions because it creates a false economy in which a demand is created for goods that are not really necessary. One only has to consider the amount of advertising for toys during children's TV programs to see this phenomenon in action. Perhaps the false economy created in this case is even more dreadful than it is normally because it incites the demand for the product in question in children, who do not have the intellectual and developmental savvy to appreciate that they are being manipulated.

However, detractors to this viewpoint would claim that advertising nevertheless does provide information about products to consumers. They assert that rather than producing a false economy, the practice of advertising helps to perpetuate competition and free enterprise in the marketplace and ultimately brings the best prices to customers. Under this view, advertising helps to sell goods to a larger market; therefore, as more goods are sold to the public, they become cheaper since they can be mass produced in order to meet demand.

But again, even a superficial analysis of this argument reveals that it is based on at least two obvious fallacies. First of all, sometimes the "information" provided in advertising is based on scant evidence, which is paraded as empirical proof in order to convince the consumer to buy. Take the advertising of cosmetics as a case in point. By now, many people will have seen the advertisement on television that states that 76% of the women tested felt that their wrinkles appeared to be visibly reduced after using a certain brand of face cream. Notice how carefully and manipulatively the advertisement is worded: "the women tested *felt* that their wrinkles *appeared* to be *visibly* reduced." The advertisement doesn't state that the condition of the women's skin actually improved from using the product. Notably, the "low price" argument also fails in this case as the women are encouraged to pay more for the product "because they're worth it."

Although I have enumerated what I see as the evils of advertising, I might be remiss if I did not concede that there is one case in which advertising does serve an extremely valuable purpose. I am speaking here about public service advertisements like those that warn against the dangers of driving while intoxicated or failing to wear a seat belt. Admittedly, these kinds of advertisements can literally have a very sobering effect.

So, what is the future of advertising? Should the government intervene to stamp down on the false or misleading claims that some advertisers attempt to make? It does in fact appear that a sea change may be beginning to take place already. For instance, some TV and magazine advertisements are now required to display footnotes at the bottom of the screen or page in order to qualify their claims. Providing information that clearly states the true limitations of products can only have a salutary effect.

Analysis of Essay Structure in Sample Essay 3

First, we will analyze the structure of the essay and the argumentative language the essay uses. On the following pages, we will analyze the writer's use of linking words, adjectives, modality, qualifiers, and verbs.

This essay uses a "scheme 1" organizational scheme.

Assertion – The primary assertion is in the last sentence of paragraph 1: "while the majority of advertising serves only to drive mindless consumerism, a certain form of advertising does, in fact, serve a useful purpose."

The argumentative language from this paragraph is: "the abundance of" and "How much of …is really useful or necessary?"

Argument 1 – The writer's first argument is in paragraph 2. It is that advertising "persuade[s] the general public to buy products that they do not need" and thereby creates a "false economy."

The argumentative language from this paragraph is: "I would argue that" and "One only has to consider."

Counterargument 1 – Counterargument 1 is in paragraph 3. It is that advertising is necessary because it "provide[s] information about products to consumers" and "brings the best prices" to them.

The argumentative language from this paragraph is: "detractors to this viewpoint would claim that," "They assert that" and "under this view."

Argument 2 – Argument 2 is in paragraph 4. It is that sometimes the information provided in advertising is misleading and that sometimes companies actually increase the prices of their products.

The argumentative language from this paragraph is: an "analysis of this argument reveals that it is based on . . . fallacies" and "Take . . . as a case in point."

In the fifth paragraph, the writer makes an exception for public service advertising.

Synthesis – The synthesis of the essay is found in the two rhetorical questions: "So, what is the future of advertising?" and "Should the government intervene to stamp down on the false or misleading claims that some advertisers attempt to make?"

Conclusion – The writer's conclusion is: "Providing information that clearly states the true limitations of products can only have a salutary effect."

Analysis of Linking Words and Verbs in Sample Essay 3

As stated in the units at the beginning of this book, you can use linking words, adjectives, modality, qualifiers, and verbs to make your ECPE essay more effective. Pay particular attention to the highlighted **linking words**, *adjectives*, and <u>verbs</u> in sample essay 3 below.

Advertising is a *powerful* force in today's materialistic, status-conscious society. Consumers are bombarded with advertising at every turn, from advertisements on television and radio, to outdoor advertising on electronic signs and even on buses. The abundance of advertising that confronts a person from one day to the next **thus** leaves one to wonder: How much of this advertising is really *useful* or *necessary*? This essay will <u>reveal</u> that **while** the majority of advertising serves only to drive *mindless* consumerism, a certain form of advertising does, **in fact**, serve a useful purpose.

Most advertising that we see nowadays, especially that on television, is the attempt of large companies to <u>persuade</u> the general public to buy products that they do not need and may not ultimately want. **In other words**, advertisements do not truly exist to give product information to consumers, **but rather** to <u>coerce</u> them mentally into buying the product in question. **Further**, I would argue that this phenomenon has larger economic repercussions **because** it creates a false economy in which a demand is created for goods that are not really necessary. One only has to consider the amount of advertising for toys during children's TV programs to see this phenomenon in action. Perhaps the false economy created in this case is even more *dreadful* than it is normally **because** it incites the demand for the product in question in children, who do not have the intellectual and developmental savvy to appreciate that they are being manipulated.

However, detractors to this viewpoint would <u>claim</u> that advertising **nevertheless** does provide information about products to consumers. They <u>assert</u> that **rather than** producing a false economy, the practice of advertising helps to <u>perpetuate</u> competition and free enterprise in the marketplace and ultimately brings the best prices to customers. **Under this view,** advertising helps to sell goods to a larger market; **therefore**, as more goods are sold to the public, they become cheaper **since** they can be mass produced in order to meet demand.

Yet again, even a superficial analysis of this argument reveals that it is based on at least two *obvious* fallacies. **First of all**, sometimes the "information" provided in advertising is based on *scant* evidence, which is paraded as empirical proof in order to <u>convince</u> the consumer to buy. Take the advertising of cosmetics as a case in point. By now, many people will have seen the advertisement on television that states that 76% of the women tested felt that their wrinkles appeared to be visibly reduced after using a certain brand of face cream. Notice how carefully and manipulatively the advertisement is worded: "the women tested felt that their wrinkles appeared to be visibly reduced." The advertisement doesn't <u>state</u> that the condition of the women's skin actually improved from using the product. Notably, the "low price" argument **also** fails in this case **as** the women are encouraged to pay more for the product "because they're worth it."

Although I have enumerated what I see as the evils of advertising, I might be remiss if I did not concede that there is one case in which advertising does serve an extremely *valuable* purpose. I am speaking here about public service advertisements like those that warn against the dangers of driving while intoxicated or failing to wear a seat belt. Admittedly, these kinds of advertisements can literally have a very sobering effect.

So, what is the future of advertising? Should the government intervene to stamp down on the false or misleading claims that some advertisers attempt to make? It does **in fact** appear that a sea change may be beginning to take place already. **For instance**, some TV and magazine advertisements are now required to display footnotes at the bottom of the screen or page in order to qualify their claims. Providing information that clearly states the true limitations of products can only have a *salutary* effect.

Analysis of Modality and Qualifiers in Sample Essay 3

Now look at essay 3 again, noting the use of <u>modality</u> and **qualifiers**.

Advertising is a powerful force in today's materialistic, status-conscious society. Consumers are bombarded with advertising at every turn, from advertisements on television and radio, to outdoor advertising on electronic signs and even on buses. The abundance of advertising that confronts a person from one day to the next thus leaves one to wonder: How much of this advertising is really useful or necessary? This essay will reveal that while the majority of advertising serves only to drive mindless consumerism, a certain form of advertising does, in fact, serve a useful purpose.

Most advertising that we see nowadays, especially that on television, is the attempt of large companies to persuade the general public to buy products that they do not need and <u>may</u> not ultimately want. In other words, advertisements do not truly exist to give product information to consumers, but rather to coerce them mentally into buying the product in question. Further, I <u>would</u> argue that this phenomenon has larger economic repercussions because it creates a false economy in which a demand is created for goods that are not really necessary. One only has to consider the amount of advertising for toys during children's TV programs to see this phenomenon in action. Perhaps the false economy created in this case is even more dreadful than it is normally because it incites the demand for the product in question in children, who do not have the intellectual and developmental savvy to appreciate that they are being manipulated.

However, detractors to this viewpoint <u>would</u> claim that advertising nevertheless does provide information about products to consumers. They assert that rather than producing a false economy, the practice of advertising helps to perpetuate competition and free enterprise in the marketplace and ultimately brings the best prices to customers. Under this view, advertising helps to sell goods to a larger market; therefore, as more goods are sold to the public, they become cheaper since they can be mass produced in order to meet demand.

Yet again, even a superficial analysis of this argument reveals that it is based on at least two obvious fallacies. First of all, sometimes the "information" provided in advertising is based on scant evidence, which is paraded as empirical proof in order to convince the consumer to buy. Take the advertising of cosmetics as a case in point. By now, many people will have seen the advertisement on television that states that 76% of the women tested felt that their wrinkles appeared to be visibly reduced after using a certain brand of face cream. Notice how carefully and manipulatively the advertisement is worded: "the women tested felt that their wrinkles appeared to be visibly reduced." The advertisement doesn't state that the condition of the women's skin actually improved from using the product. **Notably**, the "low price" argument also fails in this case as the women are encouraged to pay more for the product "because they're worth it."

Although I have enumerated what I see as the evils of advertising, I <u>might</u> be remiss if I did not concede that there is one case in which advertising does serve an extremely valuable purpose. I am speaking here about public service advertisements like those that warn against the dangers of driving while intoxicated or failing to wear a seat belt. **Admittedly**, these kinds of advertisements can literally have a very sobering effect.

So, what is the future of advertising? Should the government intervene to stamp down on the false or misleading claims that some advertisers attempt to make? It does in fact appear that a sea change may be beginning to take place already. For instance, some TV and magazine advertisements are now required to display footnotes at the bottom of the screen or page in order to qualify their claims. Providing information that clearly states the true limitations of products can only have a salutary effect.

ECPE Practice Test 4

Allow 30 minutes to take this test. A model response to the question is provided in the next section.

Answer one of the following questions:

1) The internet seems to pervade our daily lives and online searches can be useful for many tasks. Yet, some believe that the internet provides too much unreliable, useless information. Do you think that the internet provides more harm than good?

2) Some children detest attending school away from home, but others believe that boarding schools can help children to grow into well-adjusted adults. Do you think that attending boarding school is beneficial for children? Give reasons to support your opinion.

Sample Essay 4

This essay is in response to essay question 1 on the previous page. A detailed analysis of the essay is provided after the written essay response.

In today's digital and electronic age, it almost goes without question that the internet is practical for our daily lives because it makes some mundane tasks more convenient. For instance, gone are the days when one had to go to the travel agent and sit in front of a desk while the agent looked through offers on his or her screen. Internet users can now book airline tickets and make travel arrangements in the comfort of their own living rooms with the click of a mouse. But in spite of the numerous conveniences of the internet, there are those who hold the view that the internet contains a great deal of worthless, harmful, and offensive information and that the internet can be used to perpetrate deception and even crime. It appears that although the internet can be a useful tool in many ways, it needs to be used cautiously and should even be regulated, in some circumstances.

It is an undeniable facet of modern life that the internet is useful for our communication needs and for making social contacts. Remember the days when one had to post a letter to communicate with someone overseas? Those days are in the past now thanks to the wonder of e-mail, direct messaging, and social media. Still, others would maintain that often these social contacts are the breeding ground for dishonest or even criminally-minded individuals who want to prey on the weak and vulnerable. We have heard numerous stories of adolescents who are lured away from home to meet someone that they have communicated with online. Regrettably, in the end, the person making contact turns out to be a sexual predator intent on harming the young person. Such an experience certainly would negatively influence the child during the formative years of his or her personality development.

In addition to the double-edged sword effect of the communications capabilities of the internet, there is no disputing that the internet gives us ready access to a great deal of information. Indeed, some websites contain indispensable factual information for daily life and health. Consider the case of someone who wants to quit smoking. He or she can go to websites run by medical professionals to get the help and support needed to give up. Some of these types of websites are established by governmental agencies or charitable organizations, so the user can be confident that the information contained on these sites is trustworthy. On the other hand, however, one must also concede that much of the so-called "information" on the internet needs to be read with a critical mind. Since anyone can set up a website, the qualifications of the site owner, as well as the accuracy and quality of the information on the site need to be perused skeptically. The rise of medical forums run by people with no medical training whatsoever and the abundance of online shops selling discount medications are a particular worry, as some people will rely on these websites to make a self-diagnosis and then purchase medicine, without taking heed of the possibility that the medicine could potentially kill them.

Yet, others would suggest that the media has seriously exaggerated the number of incidents of internet users being grievously harmed or killed by people they have met or products they have purchased on the internet and that the very large majority of the population have the common sense to know what is dangerous or not. But what about the minority of people who do not? Will they remain unprotected just to accommodate the desires of the majority? It is true that internet usage needs to be approached vigilantly on certain occasions. The internet will need to face governmental regulation in the future, but that regulation will need to be moderate, because if the internet becomes too highly regulated, it will lose a great deal of the convenience that it already affords us.

Analysis of Essay Structure in Sample Essay 4

As before, we will analyze the structure of the essay and the argumentative language the essay uses. On the following pages, we will analyze the writer's use of linking words, adjectives, modality, qualifiers, and verbs.

This essay uses a "scheme 2" organizational scheme.

Assertion – The primary assertion is in the last sentence of paragraph 1: "although … the internet can be a useful tool in many ways, it needs to be used cautiously, and should even be regulated, in some circumstances."

The argumentative language from this paragraph is: "it almost goes without question that" and "there are those who hold the view that."

Argument 1 – The writer's first argument in paragraph 2. It is that "the internet is useful for our communication needs and for making social contacts."

Counterargument 1 – Counterargument 1 is in the second part of paragraph 2. It is that "these social contacts are the breeding ground for dishonest or even criminally-minded individuals who want to prey on the weak and vulnerable."

The argumentative language from this paragraph is: "others would maintain that" and "We have heard numerous stories of."

Argument 2 – Argument 2 is in paragraph 3. It is that "the internet gives us ready access to a great deal of information."

Counterargument 2 – Counterargument 2 is in the second half of paragraph 3. It is that "much of the so-called 'information' on the internet needs to be read with a critical mind."

The argumentative language from this paragraph is: "the double-edged sword effect of," "there is no disputing that," "Consider the case of," "one must also concede that" and "…are a particular worry."

Synthesis – The synthesis of the essay is found in the first half of the last paragraph. It is "But what about the minority of people who do not [know what is dangerous]? Will they remain unprotected just to accommodate the desires of the majority?"

Conclusion – The writer's conclusion is: "The internet will need to face governmental regulation in the future, but that regulation will need to be moderate, because if the internet becomes too highly regulated, it will lose a great deal of the convenience that it already affords us."

Analysis of Linking Words and Verbs in Sample Essay 4

Pay particular attention to the highlighted **linking words**, *adjectives*, and <u>verbs</u> in sample essay 4 below.

In today's digital and electronic age, it almost goes without question that the internet is *practical* for our daily lives because it makes some mundane tasks more convenient. **For instance**, gone are the days when one had to go to the travel agent and sit in front of a desk while the agent looked through offers on his or her screen. Internet users can now book airline tickets and make travel arrangements in the comfort of their own living rooms with the click of a mouse. **But in spite of** the numerous conveniences of the internet, there are those who <u>hold</u> the view that the internet contains a great deal of *worthless*, *harmful*, and *offensive* information and that the internet can be used to <u>perpetrate</u> deception and even crime. It appears that **although** the internet can be a *useful* tool in many ways, it needs to be used cautiously and should even be regulated, in some circumstances.

It is an *undeniable* facet of modern life that the internet is useful for our communication needs and for making social contacts. Remember the days when one had to post a letter to communicate with someone overseas? Those days are in the past now thanks to the wonder of e-mail, direct messaging, and social media. **Still**, others would <u>maintain</u> that often these social contacts are the breeding ground for *dishonest* or even *criminally-minded* individuals who want to prey on the weak and vulnerable. We have heard numerous stories of adolescents who are lured away from home to meet someone that they have communicated with online. Regrettably, in the end, the person making contact turns out to be a sexual predator intent on harming the young person. Such an experience certainly would negatively <u>influence</u> the child during the formative years of his or her personality development.

In addition to the double-edged sword effect of the communications capabilities of the internet, there is no <u>disputing</u> that the internet gives us ready access to a great deal of information. **Indeed**, some websites contain *indispensable* factual information for daily life and health. <u>Consider</u> the case of someone who wants to quit smoking. He or she can go to websites run by medical professionals to get the help and support needed to give up. Some of these types of websites are established by governmental agencies or charitable organizations, **so** the user can be confident that the information contained on these sites is *trustworthy*. **On the other hand, however**, one must also <u>concede</u> that much of the so-called "information" on the internet needs to be read with a *critical* mind. **Since** anyone can set up a website, the qualifications of the site owner, **as well as** the accuracy and quality of the information on the site need to be <u>perused</u> skeptically. The rise of medical forums run by people with no medical training whatsoever and the abundance of online shops selling discount medications are a particular worry, **as** some people will rely on these websites to make a self-diagnosis and then purchase medicine, without <u>taking heed</u> of the possibility that the medicine could potentially kill them.

Yet, others would <u>suggest</u> that the media has seriously exaggerated the number of incidents of internet users being grievously harmed or killed by people they have met or products they have purchased on the internet and that the very large majority of the population have the common sense to know what is dangerous or not. But what about the minority of people who do not? Will they remain unprotected just to accommodate the desires of the majority? It is true that internet usage needs to be approached vigilantly on certain occasions. The internet will need to face governmental regulation in the future, but that regulation would need to be *moderate*, **because** if the internet becomes too highly regulated, it will lose a great deal of the convenience that it already affords us.

Analysis of Modality and Qualifiers in Sample Essay 4

Now look at essay 4 again, noting the use of <u>modality</u> and **qualifiers**.

In today's digital and electronic age, it almost goes without question that the internet is practical for our daily lives because it makes some mundane tasks more convenient. For instance, gone are the days when one had to go to the travel agent and sit in front of a desk while the agent looked through offers on his or her screen. Internet users can now book airline tickets and make travel arrangements in the comfort of their own living rooms with the click of a mouse. But in spite of the numerous conveniences of the internet, there are those who hold the view that the internet contains a great deal of worthless, harmful, and offensive information and that the internet <u>can</u> be used to perpetrate deception and even crime. It appears that although the internet <u>can</u> be a useful tool in many ways, it needs to be used cautiously and <u>should</u> even be regulated, in some circumstances.

It is an undeniable facet of modern life that the internet is useful for our communication needs and for making social contacts. Remember the days when one had to post a letter to communicate with someone overseas? Those days are in the past now thanks to the wonder of e-mail, direct messaging, and social media. Still, others <u>would</u> maintain that often these social contacts are the breeding ground for dishonest or even criminally-minded individuals who want to prey on the weak and vulnerable. We have heard numerous stories of adolescents who are lured away from home to meet someone that they have communicated with online. **Regrettably**, in the end, the person making contact turns out to be a sexual predator intent on harming the young person. Such an experience **certainly** would negatively influence the child during the formative years of his or her personality development.

In addition to the double-edged sword effect of the communications capabilities of the internet, there is no disputing that the internet gives us ready access to a great deal of information. Indeed, some websites contain indispensable factual information for daily life and health. Consider the case of someone who wants to quit smoking. He or she can go to websites run by medical professionals to get the help and support needed to give up. Some of these types of websites are established by governmental agencies or charitable organizations, so the user can be confident that the information contained on these sites is trustworthy. On the other hand, however, one must also concede that much of the so-called "information" on the internet needs to be read with a critical mind. Since anyone can set up a website, the qualifications of the site owner, as well as the accuracy and quality of the information on the site need to be perused skeptically. The rise of medical forums run by people with no medical training whatsoever and the abundance of online shops selling discount medications are a particular worry, as some people will rely on these websites to make a self-diagnosis and then purchase medicine, without taking heed of the possibility that the medicine could potentially kill them.

Yet, others would suggest that the media has seriously exaggerated the number of incidents of internet users being grievously harmed or killed by people they have met or products they have purchased on the internet and that the very large majority of the population have the common sense to know what is dangerous or not. But what about the minority of people who do not? Will they remain unprotected just to accommodate the desires of the majority? It is true that internet usage needs to be approached vigilantly on certain occasions. The internet will need to face governmental regulation in the future, but that regulation will need to be moderate, because if the internet becomes too highly regulated, it will lose a great deal of the convenience that it already affords us.

ECPE Practice Test 5

Allow 30 minutes to take this test. A model response to the question is provided in the next section.

Answer one of the following questions.

1) Terminal cancer sufferers and other with life-ending diseases may wish to die to avoid having final days filled with pain. Do you think that euthanasia, also known as the right to die, should be considered to be a basic human right? Give reasons to support your opinion.

2) What is your response to the following statement: "Teenagers nowadays should be required to do a stint of manual labor to show them what a hard day's work is." Give reasons to support your opinion.

Sample Essay 5

This essay is in response to essay question 1 on the previous page. A detailed analysis of the essay is provided after the written essay response.

Modern advancements in science and medicine have meant that life expectancy is much longer now than in the past. A number of previously fatal conditions and illness, such as having the HIV virus, can now be addressed with the use of medications and other treatments because of modern science. Yet, in some cases, the life that the seriously ill person lives is full of pain and suffering. Would it be more humane in these cases to permit euthanasia? The choice about receiving medical treatment or not during life-threatening conditions is one that ought to be very strictly controlled and is one that can be answered competently only if we first respond to two other questions: Who should decide what the best course of action is in each individual case and under what conditions?

Clearly, pain and suffering are very individual and private experiences as each person has a very different threshold for and tolerance of pain. Patients who have been diagnosed with terminal, incurable illnesses and have been given months to live might prefer not to live during those remaining months if there is going to be a great deal of intense suffering. In essence, the question revolves around the quality of the patient's remaining life. Nevertheless, opponents to this viewpoint are quick to point out that misdiagnoses are made and that patients do sometimes make unexplained recoveries after having received grim prognoses. But experience tells us that this is normally not the case: miraculous recoveries are few and far between in reality, and having false hope generally only works to prolong suffering and a poor quality of life.

The "quality of life" argument is particularly persuasive when the patient shows no brain activity and is being kept alive on a life-support machine. If our loved one is mentally incapacitated, he or she cannot make a decision about his or her own welfare. Who then should? Is it right for family members to decide? The problem is that family members, already struggling to come to terms with their loved one's grave condition, are now placed in the unenviable position of having to make an agonizing choice. They may ask themselves what their loved one would have wanted, but in the end, such decisions are made under great mental duress and may be decisions that the family members ultimately live to regret.

However, the argument above is based on the presumption that the family relationship is amicable and that family members will always place a priority on the wishes of their loved one. What happens when this is not the case? In the most extreme case, this argument holds that family members might act to hasten the death of the patient in order to put an end to an acrimonious family life, to be able to collect inheritance and insurance pay-outs, or both. Avarice, they claim, is a more powerful human motivator than love, so consider the power of greed when love has ceased to exist. Surely, they assert, we should not let those who stand to gain from the patient's death make the very decision that the patient should die.

In order to attempt to address the murky issues surrounding euthanasia, several countries are now recognizing Advance Health Directives as a matter of law. The directive, which the individual must make when he or she is of sound mind, stipulates the conditions for the receipt of medical treatment and hospital care. The legal document must be signed and sworn and is valid only when and if the person giving the directive is unable to provide consent because of mental incapacity. Such a document effectively removes the need for family members to ponder the wishes of the patient since the patient has already committed his or her wishes to writing. The document also protects the patient in the event that unscrupulous family members may want to hasten the patient's death for personal or financial reasons. While the debate about euthanasia *per se* might continue in cases where the patient has not expressed his or her wishes beforehand, Advance Health Directives are certainly a positive step in addressing the issue.

Analysis of Essay Structure in Sample Essay 5

The structure of the essay and the argumentative language the essay uses are analyzed below. On the following pages, the writer's use of linking words, adjectives, modality, qualifiers, and verbs is analyzed.

This essay uses a "scheme 2" organizational scheme.

Assertion – The primary assertion is in the last sentence of paragraph 1: "The choice about receiving medical treatment or not during life-threatening conditions is one that ought to be very strictly controlled and is one that can be answered competently only if we first respond to two other questions: Who should decide what the best course of action is in each individual case and under what conditions?"

The argumentative language from this paragraph is: "have meant that" and "in some cases."

Argument 1 – The writer's first argument in paragraph 2. It is that "Patients who have been diagnosed with terminal, incurable illnesses and have been given months to live might prefer not to live during those remaining months if there is going to be a great deal of intense suffering."

Counterargument 1 – Counterargument 1 is in the second half of paragraph 2. It is that "misdiagnoses are made and that patients do sometimes make unexplained recoveries after having received grim prognoses."

The argumentative language from this paragraph is: "the question revolves around," "opponents to this viewpoint," "experience tells us that," and "in reality."

Argument 2 – Argument 2 is in paragraph 3. It is that the "'quality of life" argument is particularly persuasive when the patient shows no brain activity and is being kept alive on a life support machine."

The argumentative language from this paragraph is: "argument is particularly persuasive when," "Is it right for … to …?," "The problem is that" and "They may ask themselves."

Counterargument 2 – Counterargument 2 is in paragraph 4. It is that there are flaws in the argument that "the family relationship is amicable and that family members will always place a priority on the wishes of their loved one."

The argumentative language from this paragraph is: "the argument above is based on the presumption that…," "What happens when this is not the case?," "In the most extreme case," "this argument holds that…," "they claim," "so consider" and "they assert."

Synthesis – The synthesis of the essay is found in the last paragraph. It is that "In order to attempt to address the murky issues surrounding euthanasia, several countries are now recognizing Advance Health Directives as a matter of law."

Conclusion – The writer's conclusion is: "While the debate about euthanasia *per se* might continue in cases where the patient has not expressed his or her wishes beforehand, Advance Health Directives are certainly a positive step in addressing the issue."

Analysis of Linking Words and Verbs in Sample Essay 5

Pay particular attention to the highlighted **linking words**, *adjectives*, and verbs in sample essay 5 below.

Modern advancements in science and medicine have meant that life expectancy is much longer now than in the past. A number of previously fatal conditions and illness, such as having the HIV virus, can now be addressed with the use of medications and other treatments because of modern science. **Yet**, in some cases, the life that the seriously ill person lives is full of pain and suffering. Would it be more humane in these cases to permit euthanasia? The choice about receiving medical treatment or not during life-threatening conditions is one that ought to be very strictly controlled and is one that can be answered competently only if we **first** respond to two other questions: Who should decide what the *best* course of action is in each individual case and under what conditions?

Clearly, pain and suffering are very *individual* and *private* experiences as each person has a very *different* threshold for and tolerance of pain. Patients who have been diagnosed with terminal, incurable illnesses and have been given months to live might prefer not to live during those remaining months if there is going to be a great deal of *intense* suffering. **In essence**, the question revolves around the quality of the patient's remaining life. **Nevertheless**, opponents to this viewpoint are quick to point out that misdiagnoses are made and that patients do sometimes make unexplained recoveries after having received *grim* prognoses. But experience tells us that this is normally not the case: miraculous recoveries are few and far between in reality, and having false hope generally only works to prolong suffering and a *poor* quality of life.

The "quality of life" argument is particularly *persuasive* **when** the patient shows no brain activity and is being kept alive on a life-support machine. If our loved one is mentally incapacitated, he or she cannot make a decision about his or her own welfare. Who then should? Is it right for family members to decide? The problem is that family members, already struggling to come to terms with their loved one's *grave* condition, are now placed in the *unenviable* position of having to make an *agonizing* choice. They may ask themselves what their loved one would have wanted, but in the end, such decisions are made under great mental duress and may be decisions that the family members ultimately live to regret.

However, the argument above is based on the presumption that the family relationship is *amicable* and that family members will always place a priority on the wishes of their loved one. What happens when this is not the case? In the most extreme case, this argument holds that family members might act to hasten the death of the patient in order to put an end to an *acrimonious* family life, to be able to collect inheritance and insurance pay-outs, or both. Avarice, they claim, is a more powerful human motivator than love, **so** consider the power of greed when love has ceased to exist. Surely, they assert, we should not let those who stand to gain from the patient's death make the very decision that the patient should die.

In order to attempt to address the *murky* issues surrounding euthanasia, several countries are now recognizing Advance Health Directives as a matter of law. The directive, which the individual must make when he or she is of sound mind, stipulates the conditions for the receipt of medical treatment and hospital care. The legal document must be signed and sworn and is valid only when and if the person giving the directive is unable to provide consent **because of** mental incapacity. Such a document effectively removes the need for family members to ponder the wishes of the patient **since** the patient has already committed his or her wishes to writing. The document **also** protects the patient in the event that *unscrupulous* family members may want to hasten the patient's death for personal or financial reasons. **While** the debate about euthanasia per se might continue in cases where the patient has not expressed his or her wishes beforehand, Advance Health Directives are certainly a *positive* step in addressing the issue.

Analysis of Modality and Qualifiers in Sample Essay 5

Now look at essay 5 again, noting the use of <u>modality</u> and **qualifiers**.

Modern advancements in science and medicine have meant that life expectancy is much longer now than in the past. A number of previously fatal conditions and illness, such as having the HIV virus, can now be addressed with the use of medications and other treatments because of modern science. Yet, in some cases, the life that the seriously ill person lives is full of pain and suffering. <u>Would</u> it be more humane in these cases to permit euthanasia? The choice about receiving medical treatment or not during life-threatening conditions is one that <u>ought</u> to be very strictly controlled and is one that can be answered competently only if we first respond to two other questions: Who <u>should</u> decide what the best course of action is in each individual case and under what conditions?

Clearly, pain and suffering are very individual and private experiences as each person has a very different threshold for and tolerance of pain. Patients who have been diagnosed with terminal, incurable illnesses and have been given months to live <u>might</u> prefer not to live during those remaining months if there is going to be a great deal of intense suffering. In essence, the question revolves around the quality of the patient's remaining life. Nevertheless, opponents to this viewpoint are quick to point out that misdiagnoses are made and that patients do sometimes make unexplained recoveries after having received grim prognoses. But experience tells us that this is normally not the case: miraculous recoveries are few and far between in reality, and having false hope generally only works to prolong suffering and a poor quality of life.

The "quality of life" argument is **particularly** persuasive when the patient shows no brain activity and is being kept alive on a life-support machine. If our loved one is mentally incapacitated, he or she cannot make a decision about his or her own welfare. Who then should? Is it right for family members to decide? The problem is that family members, already struggling to come to terms with their loved one's grave condition, are now placed in the unenviable position of having to make an agonizing choice. They may ask themselves what their loved one would have wanted, but in the end, such decisions are made under great mental duress and may be decisions that the family members ultimately live to regret.

However, the argument above is based on the presumption that the family relationship is amicable and that family members will always place a priority on the wishes of their loved one. What happens when this is not the case? In the most extreme case, this argument holds that family members might act to hasten the death of the patient in order to put an end to an acrimonious family life, to be able to collect inheritance and insurance pay-outs, or both. Avarice, they claim, is a more powerful human motivator than love, so consider the power of greed when love has ceased to exist. Surely, they assert, we should not let those who stand to gain from the patient's death make the very decision that the patient should die.

In order to attempt to address the murky issues surrounding euthanasia, several countries are now recognizing Advance Health Directives as a matter of law. The directive, which the individual <u>must</u> make when he or she is of sound mind, stipulates the conditions for the receipt of medical treatment and hospital care. The legal document <u>must</u> be signed and sworn and is valid only when and if the person giving the directive is unable to provide consent because of mental incapacity. Such a document effectively removes the need for family members to ponder the wishes of the patient since the patient has already committed his or her wishes to writing. The document also protects the patient in the event that unscrupulous family members <u>may</u> want to hasten the patient's death for personal or financial reasons. While the debate about euthanasia per se <u>might</u> continue in cases where the patient has not expressed his or her wishes beforehand, Advance Health Directives are **certainly** a positive step in addressing the issue.

Vocabulary for the ECPE Essay – Using the Academic Word List

This study guide has covered the various aspects of grammar and structure that you need to demonstrate in your essay.

However, the examiner also assesses your vocabulary level as he or she reads through the various paragraphs of your essay.

The following pages contain a list of academic words. You should study the list and try to use these words in your ECPE essay.

Academic Word List

abundant	appropriate
acceptability	approve
acceptable	arguably
access	argue
accessibility	aspect
accessible	atrocity
accumulate	attribute
accurate	believe
acknowledge	capacity
acquire	catalyst
admit	category
adversity	caveat
advocate	circumstance
affirm	cite
aggregate	claim
agitate	clarify
agitation	codify
analogy	coherent
announce	comment
approbation	communicate

compile	criteria
compose	crucial
comprehensive	decline
conclude	deduce
concurrent	demonstrate
conduct	deny
confirm	despotic
consider	determine
consist	deterrent
constitute	derive
construct	deviate
consult	differentiate
contemplate	diminish
contradict	discern
contravene	discipline
controversy	discriminate
convenient	dispose
convention	dispute
conventional	distribute
convey	diverse
create	document
credence	dominate

drawback	exploit
eliminate	extract
emerge	facilitate
emphasize	factor
empirical	feature
encounter	fluctuate
enforce	focus
enhance	formula
enumerate	foundation
environment	framework
equate	fundamental
equivalent	general
erode	generate
establish	grant
estimate	gratification
evaluate	gratify
evident	guideline
exhibit	heinous
exist	hierarchy
existence	highlight
experience	hypothesis
explicit	identify

ideology	inspect
illustrate	instance
immense	instruct
impact	integral
implement	integrity
implicate	intense
imply	interact
inappropriate	interpret
incentive	intervene
incidence	intrinsic
indicate	investigate
individual	invoke
induce	involve
inevitable	ironically
infer	irretrievable
inflection	isolate
inhabitant	issue
inherent	item
innovate	judgment
input	justify
insidious	labor
insight	legislate

levy	network
liberal	neutral
literal	norm
locate	notion
logic	nuance
maintain	objective
major	observe
manipulate	obtain
maximize	occasion
mechanism	occupy
media	occur
mediate	offender
method	offset
minimize	ongoing
misconstrue	option
misfortune	outcome
misinterpret	oversee
mode	paradigm
modify	parallel
motive	parameter
mutual	participate
negate	perceive

persecute

perspective

phenomenon

philosophy

policy

possession

postulate

potential

precede

precise

predict

predominant

preliminary

presume

previous

primary

principal

priority

process

professional

prohibit

promote

proportion

propose

prospect

protocol

publication

purchase

pursue

quote

rational

recipient

recover

refine

refute

regime

register

regrettable

regulate

reinforce

reject

release

relevant

reluctant

remarkable	select
repudiate	sequence
require	shortcoming
research	significant
reside	situation
resolve	specific
resource	specify
respond	statistic
restore	status
restrain	stipulate
restrict	straightforward
restriction	strategy
reveal	stricken
revenue	structure
reverse	submit
revise	subordinate
satisfaction	subsequent
satisfy	subtlety
scenario	sufficient
schadenfreude	summary
scheme	supplement
scope	surrender

survey

suspend

sustain

technique

technology

terminate

theory

transform

ultimate

ultimatum

undergo

underlie

undertake

unfortunate

uniform

unimaginable

unique

unthinkable

untoward

utilize

utter

utterance

valid

vary

version

widespread

would-be

wrongdoing

ECPE Essay Writing – Practice Test Questions

1. Many people believe in the expression: "An eye for an eye; a tooth for a tooth." Likewise, they believe that murderers should be put to death for the crimes they commit. What is your response to the view that the death penalty should be reinstated for all those convicted of murder?

2. The government should do more to address the issue of domestic violence. Do you agree? Give reasons to support your opinion.

3. Whether to be used for recreation of for pain relief, marijuana can be purchased in stores legally in some states. Some belief that marijuana should be fully legalized in all states, while others have serious reservations about this idea. What do you think that are the advantages and disadvantages of legalizing marijuana?

4. Society is becoming increasingly reliant on computers for communication. Is this a good thing?

5. Censorship in printed and digital media should be considered a necessary evil. Do you agree? Give reasons to support your opinion.

6. Cosmetic surgery has recently become big business. Yet, some cosmetic surgeons are not licensed to conduct the operations that they perform on their patients. What is your response to the view that the government should intervene to regulate cosmetic surgery?

7. Society should assume more responsibility for pregnant teenagers and the children they bear. Do you agree? Give reasons to support your opinion.

8. The ban on cigarette smoking in public places should be repealed as it is yet another example of the over-involvement of governmental regulation in our daily lives. What are the advantages and disadvantages of the ban on cigarette smoking in public places?

9. All animal testing for scientific reasons should be banned. Do you agree? Give reasons to support your opinion.

10. The census has revealed that many families regularly overspend. However, some families could not live day to day without going into debt. What is your response to the view that people should spend less on credit? Give reasons and examples to support your opinion.

Using Correct Grammar and Punctuation

Mechanical conventions are the rules of grammar and punctuation that are necessary in order to write accurately and correctly.

This section is intended as a basic overview of some of the most important mechanical conventions for the exam.

Comparatives and Superlatives – Avoid Using Double Forms:

Use the comparative form when comparing two things.

The comparative form consists of the adjective plus –er when the adjective has two syllables or less.

pretty → prettier

Avoid making a double comparative:

INCORRECT: more prettier

When the adjective has more than two syllables, the adjective should be preceded by the word "more" in order to form the comparative.

beautiful → more beautiful

Examples:

Tom is taller than his brother.

Tom is more intelligent than his brother.

If you are comparing more than two things, you must use the superlative form.

As a general rule, the superlative form consists of the adjective plus –est when the adjective has two syllables or less.

pretty → prettiest

Avoid making a double superlative:

INCORRECT: most prettiest

To form the superlative for adjectives that have more than two syllables, the adjective should be preceded by the word "most".

beautiful → most beautiful

Examples:

Tom is the tallest boy in his class.

Tom is the most intelligent boy in his class.

Correct Use of *Its* and *It's*:

"Its" is a possessive pronoun, while "it's" is a contraction of "it is."

CORRECT: It's high time you started to study.

INCORRECT: Its high time you started to study.

The sentence could also be stated as follows: It is high time that you started to study.

Since the contracted form of "it is" is used in the alternative sentence, "it's" is the correct form.

CORRECT: A snake sheds its skin at least once a year.

INCORRECT: A snake sheds it's skin at least once a year.

"Its" is a possessive pronoun referring to the snake, so the apostrophe should not be used.

Correct Use of *Their*, *There*, and *They're*:

"Their" is a plural possessive pronoun.

"There" is used to describe the location of something.

"They're" is a contraction of "they are."

CORRECT: Their house is made of brick and concrete.

INCORRECT: There house is made of brick and concrete.

INCORRECT: They're house is made of brick and concrete.

In this case, "their" is the possessive pronoun explaining to whom the house belongs.

CORRECT: He attended college with his cousins living there in California.

INCORRECT: He attended college with his cousins living their in California.

INCORRECT: He attended college with his cousins living they're in California.

"There" is referring to the state of California in the example above, so it is used to talk about the location.

CORRECT: They're away on vacation at the moment.

INCORRECT: Their away on vacation at the moment.

INCORRECT: There away on vacation at the moment.

The sentence could also be written as follows: They are away on vacation at the moment.

"They're" is a contraction of "they are," so the apostrophe needs to be used.

Correct Use of *Were*, *Where*, and *We're*:

"Were" is the past tense of the verb "are."

"Where" is used to inquire about or describe the location of something.

"We're" is a contraction of "we are."

CORRECT: They were going to call you, but the phone was out of order.

INCORRECT: They where going to call you, but the phone was out of order.

INCORRECT: They we're going to call you, but the phone was out of order.

"Were" is the past form of the verb in the sentence above.

CORRECT: Where is the mall located?

INCORRECT: Were is the mall located?

INCORRECT: We're is the mall located?

"Where" needs to be used because the sentence is making an inquiry about the location of the mall.

CORRECT: We're so happy that you got accepted into college.

INCORRECT: Were so happy that you got accepted into college.

INCORRECT: Where so happy that you got accepted into college.

The sentence could be written as follows: We are so happy that you got accepted into college.

"We're" is a contraction of "we are," so the apostrophe needs to be used.

Avoid the "is where" construction:

CORRECT: An identity crisis, which is the experience of confusion about one's life goals and ambitions, often occurs in middle age.

INCORRECT: An identity crisis is where there is the experience of confusion about one's life goals and ambitions, and it often occurs in middle age.

The construction in the second sentence may be used in informal speaking, but such constructions should be avoided in your essay.

Misplaced Modifiers:

Modifiers are phrases that describe other parts of a sentence. The modifier should always be placed directly before or after the noun to which it relates. Now look at these examples:

CORRECT: Like Minnesota, Wisconsin gets extremely cold in the winter.

INCORRECT: Like Minnesota, it gets extremely cold in Wisconsin in the winter.

The phrase "like Minnesota" is an adjectival phrase that modifies the noun "Wisconsin."

Therefore, "Wisconsin" must come directly after the comma.

Here are two more examples:

CORRECT: While at the mall, a gang of youths committed a robbery.

INCORRECT: While at the mall, a robbery was committed.

The adverbial phrase "while at the mall" modifies the noun phrase "a gang of youths," so this noun phrase needs to come after the adverbial phrase.

Parallelism:

When giving items in a series, be sure to use consistent forms.

CORRECT: The position involves answering phone calls, writing letters, and getting supplies.

INCORRECT: The position involves answering phone calls, writing letters, and get supplies.

All of the items in the series should be in the –ing form.

CORRECT: I saw Tom's accident yesterday, and I tried to help.

INCORRECT: I saw Tom's accident yesterday, and I try to help.

Both parts of the sentence are describing actions that occurred yesterday, so the past tense (–ed) needs to be used for both verbs.

Punctuation and Independent Clauses – Avoiding Run-On Sentences:

Run-on sentences are those that use commas to join independent clauses together, instead of correctly using the period.

An independent clause contains a grammatical subject and verb. It therefore can stand alone as its own sentence.

The first word of the independent clause should begin with a capital letter, and the clause should be preceded by a period.

CORRECT: I thought I would live in this city forever. Then I lost my job.

INCORRECT: I thought I would live in this city forever, then I lost my job.

"Then I lost my job" is a complete sentence. It has a grammatical subject (I) and a verb (lost). The independent clause must be preceded by a period, and the first word of the new sentence must begin with a capital letter.

Alternatively, an appropriate conjunction can be used to join the independent clauses:

I thought I would live in this city forever, and then I lost my job.

Punctuation and Quotation Marks:

Punctuation should be enclosed within the final quotation mark when giving dialogue.

CORRECT: "I can't believe you bought a new car," Sam remarked.

INCORRECT: "I can't believe you bought a new car", Sam remarked.

In the example below, the word "exclaimed" shows that the exclamation point is needed.

CORRECT: "I can't believe you bought a new car!" Sam exclaimed.

INCORRECT: "I can't believe you bought a new car"! Sam exclaimed.

However, if the quotation is stated indirectly, no quotation marks should be used.

CORRECT: Sam exclaimed that he couldn't believe that I had bought a new car.

INCORRECT: Sam exclaimed that "he couldn't believe that I had bought a new car."

Punctuation for Items in a Series:

When using "and" and "or" for more than two items in a series, be sure to use the comma before the words "and" and "or."

CORRECT: You need to bring a tent, sleeping bag, and flashlight.

INCORRECT: You need to bring a tent, sleeping bag and flashlight.

Notice the use of the comma after the word "bag" and before the word "and" in the series.

CORRECT: Students can call, write a letter, or send an email.

INCORRECT: Students can call, write a letter or send an email.

Notice the use of the comma after the word "letter" and before the word "or" in the series.

Restrictive and Non-restrictive Modifiers:

Restrictive modifiers are clauses or phrases that provide essential information in order to identify the grammatical subject. Restrictive modifiers should not be preceded by a comma.

<u>Example:</u> My sister who lives in Indianapolis is a good swimmer.

In this case, the speaker has more than one sister, and she is identifying which sister she is talking about by giving the essential information "who lives in Indianapolis."

On the other hand, a non-restrictive modifier is a clause or phrase that provides extra information about a grammatical subject in a sentence. A non-restrictive modifier must be preceded by a comma.

Non-restrictive modifiers are also known as non-essential modifiers.

Example: My sister, who lives in Indianapolis, is a good swimmer.

In this case, the speaker has only one sister. Therefore, the information about her sister's city of residence is not essential in order to identify which sister she is talking about.

The words "who lives in Indianapolis" form a non-restrictive modifier.

Sentence Fragments:

A sentence fragment is a group of words that does not express a complete train of thought.

CORRECT: I like Denver because it has a great university.

INCORRECT: I like Denver. Because it has a great university.

In the second example, "because it has a great university" is not a complete thought. This idea needs to be joined with the previous clause in order to be grammatically correct.

Subject-Verb Agreement:

Subjects must agree with verbs in number.

Subject-verb agreement can be confusing when there are intervening words in a sentence.

CORRECT: The flowers in the pots in the garden grow quickly.

INCORRECT: The flowers in the pots in the garden grows quickly.

The grammatical subject in the above sentence is "flowers," not "garden," so the plural form of the verb (*grow*) needs to be used.

CORRECT: Each person in the groups of students needs to pay attention to the instructions.

INCORRECT: Each person in the groups of students need to pay attention to the instructions.

The grammatical subject in the above sentence is "each person," not "students." "Each" is singular and therefore needs the singular form of the verb (*needs*).

Using Correct Grammar and Punctuation – Exercises

Each of the sentences below has problems with grammar and punctuation. Find the errors in the sentences and correct them. You may wish to refer to the advice in the previous section as you do the exercise.
The answers are provided on the page following the exercises.

1) I haven't seen her or her sister. Since they went away to college.

2) People who like to get up early in the morning in order to drink more coffee is likely to become easily tired in the afternoon.

3) Were we're you when we called you yesterday?

4) She is the most happiest person that I know.

5) Hanging from the knob on the bedroom door, Tom thought the new shirt was his favorite.

6) I ran across the street to speak to her, then she surprised me by saying "that she had bought a new car."

7) Its common for a magazine to have better sales if it mentions computers, handhelds or other new technology on it's cover.

8) After losing long-term employment, many people suffer from anxiety, loneliness and get depressed.

9) Each student in the class who will take the series of exams on advanced mathematics need to study in advance.

10) Their are several reasons why there having problems with they're children.

Using Correct Grammar and Punctuation – Answers

1) I haven't seen her or her sister since they went away to college.

2) People who like to get up early in the morning in order to drink more coffee are likely to become easily tired in the afternoon.

3) Where were you when we called you yesterday?

4) She is the happiest person that I know.

5) Hanging from the knob on the bedroom door, the new shirt was Tom's favorite.

6) I ran across the street to speak to her. Then she surprised me by saying that she had bought a new car.

7) It's common for a magazine to have better sales if it mentions computers, handhelds, or other new technology on its cover.

8) After losing long-term employment, many people suffer from anxiety, loneliness, and depression.

9) Each student in the class who will take the series of exams on advanced mathematics needs to study in advance.

10) There are several reasons why they're having problems with their children.

www.ingramcontent.com/pod-product-compliance
Lightning Source LLC
Chambersburg PA
CBHW081751100526
44592CB00015B/2385